H'mong Batik

A Textile Technique From Laos

Jane Mallinson, Nancy Donnelly, and Ly Hang

Drawings by
**Margaret Davidson, Mai Ying Her,
Mang Vang, La Xiong,
and Blia Hang Yang**

D1614074

University of Washington Press
Seattle and London

Copyright © 1988 by Mallinson and Donnelly

First Thailand edition published by Silkworm Books in 1996
First University of Washington Press edition published in 1997

ISBN 0-295-97054-5

Printed in Thailand by O.S. Printing House, Bangkok

Cover illustration: This pattern is often called "divorce," because it is relatively easy and quick
to do. The story goes that a woman married a man whose mother was a batik artist. But because
the woman was not happy, and did not behave like a good wife, her mother-in-law refused to
teach her batik. The woman wanted to learn to make herself a skirt so she could go to the New
Year's party and find another husband. Since her mother-in-law would not teach her, she
watched over the other women making batik, then went home, got a pen, some wax, and some
cloth, and taught herself a very simple pattern. She made a skirt, and got her divorce. H'mong
women laugh at the name, but often use the pattern for its speed, particularly for everyday
"feeding the pigs and chickens" skirts. It is also one of the first patterns taught to young girls.

Acknowledgments

The authors would like to thank Margaret Davidson, Mady Deutsch, Kim Field, Jerry Gold, Nhia Doua Hang, Sao Hang, Mai Ying Her, Philip Mallinson, Patricia Symonds, Mang Vang, La Xiong and Blia Hang Yang for varied and essential assistance without any element of which the project would have foundered. We are also grateful to the Social Science Research Council of New York, for grant support during part of the information gathering phase of the project.

A Blue H'mong woman in traditional costume in Laos.

A Note on the Illustrations

In collecting the patterns for this book, we limited ourselves, for clarity, to pen drawings of designs, or to the waxed cloth. We did not get dyed pieces because the women with whom we were working had either given up dyeing in the United States, or had had such poor luck with the unfamiliar dyes that they could not be sure of getting clear designs at the end of the process. So in making the illustrations for this book we have completed the process, technologically. We have taken the drawings or waxed cloth, photographed them, reversed the negatives, and printed them so that the picture you see looks like the ideal, finished indigo-dyed pattern, with the waxed lines showing the white pattern against a background of dark blue.

The captions include all the information given by each artist about her particular pattern. In some cases this was just a short title; in others, it was a long, sometimes rambling description of individual motifs.

The work of four artists is represented: Mang Vang and La Xiong from Sayaboury, and Blia Hang Yang and Mai Ying Her from Xieng Khouang. Mang Vang and La Xiong have signed each of their patterns; of the others, the waxed patterns are the work of Blia Hang Yang, while the pen drawings are the work of Mai Ying Her.

Mang Vang and La Xiong knew each other well in Laos, where La Xiong, who is slightly older, taught Mang Vang many of her patterns. Mang Vang now lives in Washington, while La Xiong, Blia Hang Yang and Mai Ying Her all live in California.

vi

Table of Contents

A Brief History of the H'mong 1

Textiles and H'mong Society 29

Learning To Do Batik 41

Textiles as Costume — Women's Dress 49

The Making of a Batik Skirt 53

Recent Developments and Innovations in Blue H'mong Skirts 75

Story: The Origin of Batik 77

Bibliography for Further Reading 83

Authors 87

Map of Laos showing the four northern provinces where most of the H'mong live: Sayaboury, Sam Neua, Xieng Khouang, and Luang Prabang. The artists of this book came from Sayaboury Province and Xieng Khouang Provivince.

China

Burma

Vietnam

Luang Prabang

Sam Neua

Mekong River

Luang Prabang

Xieng Khouang

Sayaboury

Xieng Khouang

Gulf of Tonkin

Vang Vieng

Sayaboury

Vientiane

Thailand

Mekong River

LAOS

——— Boundary of Laos
——— Other International Boundary
–·–·– Provincial Boundary
◉ National Capital
• Provincial Capital

100 miles
100 kilometers

Mekong River

Drawn from a map by Dr. Joel Halpern

Cambodia

A Brief History of the H'mong

The H'mong began as a small group in an area that later became part of China. In the valley of the Yangtse River, they began to take on their identity as a separate people with particular cultural practices and social structure. They are first mentioned historically in Chinese chronicles over 2,500 years ago, but references to them are sparse and sporadic for many centuries. We cannot be sure that every mention of "Miao" (the Chinese name for the H'mong) actually refers to the same group we now call H'mong.

The Chinese chronicles consider the H'mong to be outsiders and dangerous, barbarian people, but this attitude probably sprang from a profound misunderstanding of the H'mong people, who were living in areas where the Chinese wanted to expand their political and military control. As the Chinese pushed the H'mong ever southward into increasingly mountainous territory, the H'mong saw that in the highlands they could be safe and independent. Armies seeking to expand the borders of the Chinese state were baffled by the hilly terrain. Today H'mong celebrate the isolation of mountain life in their stories and songs; they attribute health to mountain

*A New Year's pattern with
shells and cats' feet.*
Mang Vang

coolness and fresh air. The H'mong continue to be identified with upland areas, for throughout Asia they generally live above 5,000 feet.

After 1800, some H'mong began migrating southward out of China, owing in part to increasing efforts by the Chinese to tax them. By 1900, H'mong had begun displacing other highland groups in areas of Southeast Asia close to China, and by 1975 an estimated 293,000 were living in Laos. The French colonial presence in lowland Laos, which had begun in 1893, extended into the highlands by 1920, and the French troops found themselves confronting a H'mong uprising (the *Rog Vwm*, or so-called "Crazy War," 1919-1921). Though the H'mong were unable to repel the French, they successfully retained their traditional independence from lowland Lao and Vietnamese by negotiating direct relations with the French colonial superstructure. This quasi-independence continued through the colonial period.

The H'mong in the past had deliberately set themselves apart from other groups in China and Southeast Asia. H'mong could be identified at a glance among the mosaic of tribes in upland Laos by their clothing, with its particular cut and elaborate, abstract embroidery, applique, or batik. All writers on H'mong mention costume as an element of ethnic identity.

Confining their living places to high altitudes, wearing their distinctive clothing, following their own ritual practices, H'mong organized themselves for nearly self-sufficient production, and avoided political entanglements with other groups insofar as possible. However, as the colonial power of France grew in Indochina, the

Each group is a pair of families, a mother and father (circles) and two children (shells).
Mang Vang

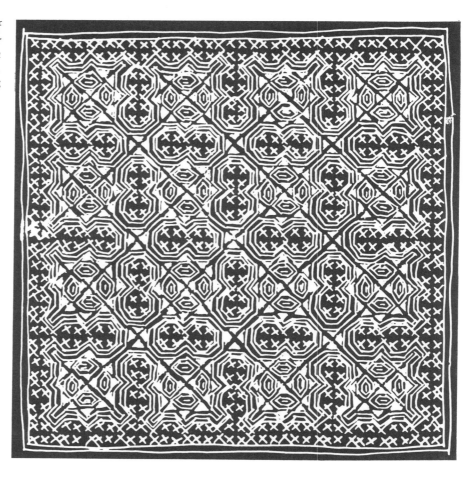

Thai nation-state also extended its own reach, to protect its borders. During the 20th century, especially as travel and communications became more efficient, centralizing governments have reached farther and farther into the hinterlands and the scope of H'mong independence has shrunk.

* * *

Before 1950, life for H'mong in Laos was agricultural, with essentially all H'mong scattered in small hamlets high in the hills. They used slash and burn methods to grow upland rice, corn, squash, cucumbers, mustard, and opium poppies, moving to new land as soils became exhausted, and they also raised pigs, chickens, horses, and cattle. The major cash crop was opium, packed out by horse and traded for silver. Most contacts with non-H'mong occurred through trade. Only men engaged in trade, so that all the silver, including women's jewelry made from French-Indochinese piastres, was always considered the property of men.

Because agriculture was not based on land passed from father to son but on land worked to exhaustion and then abandoned for freshly cleared land, households and indeed whole villages moved from time to time. Continued association between male household members, especially after moves, was not based on inherited patrimony (as with the Chinese) but on a continued desire to associate with each other.

"The circles and the shells are the people, everyone is living together" surrounded by cucumber seeds and cat footprints.
Mang Vang

Egalitarianism and freedom of choice by the head of each family regarding where to live and whom to live with were important social values. Still, several factors tended to pull related families together into group households. Farming was more efficient with many workers. H'mong families were also bound together by a requirement for ancestor worship in the male line. Particularly close relationships were strongly valued between brothers and male cousins. So ritual and emotional ties as well as production considerations tended to keep brothers within a single household.

Within such an extended household, each nuclear family occupied a separate bedroom. Household chores and agricultural labor were undertaken together under the supervision of the senior couple. Farm technology was very simple. With most land at a fifteen- to thirty-degree slope, machinery, plows, and even wheeled vehicles were impractical. The main tools were knives, short-handled hoes, and digging sticks. Harvests had to be carried on the backs of people or horses. In short, farm production was difficult and productivity was rather low. If many children were born, their number quickly exceeded the capacity of their parents to feed them. But if many adults remained under one roof, household tasks in particular could be handled more efficiently. This freed most women for farm work alongside the men, increasing production.

The ideal household size was as large as possible, with polygyny being acceptable and frequent childbirth expected. The household cycle would begin with mature brothers, each with at least one wife and several children, splitting their common

"The parents (circles) are in the middle, the babies (shells) are around them" with a border of cucumber seeds.
Mang Vang

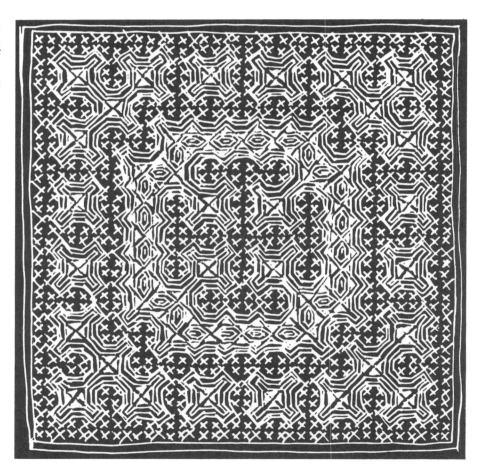

household and forming separate nuclear households. This would be most likely to happen after the death of their father, although if they quarreled one or more might split off earlier. The oldest surviving parent would usually live with the youngest married son, and any unmarried brothers or sisters would stay with one of the married brothers. As time passed and the new generation of children grew up, daughters married out and sons brought wives in, forming new extended households that continued until again the sons decided to separate into nuclear households. Not all families underwent this years-long process, but enough did that it became the expected norm.

H'mong women in Laos wanted many children. Their desire came partly from cultural factors: maturity for both men and women was figured in terms of parenthood, and sons were needed to perpetuate the patrilineal family. But the need for economic survival in old age also spurred women toward pregnancy. Many children, though burdensome in early childhood, were a necessity later in life, for they were the only form of social insurance in the mountains of Laos. In fact, only sons "counted" toward potential support in old age, because daughters married into other families.

A related reason for the strong desire of H'mong women in Laos to bear many children was the high death rate among children under five. Donnelly asked eight refugee H'mong women from various places in Laos to reconstruct their family trees, and found that approximately half of all the children reported born to three generations of these families had died before their fifth year, from disease, accident, or war.

"Pumpkin flowers in the street."
Mang Vang

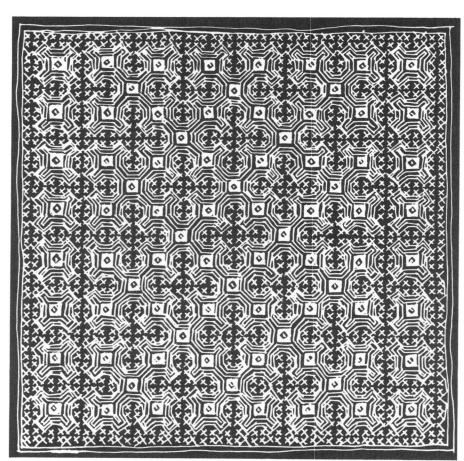

Geddes reported crude birthrates ranging from 49 to 76 births per year per 1,000 women aged 15-45 among H'mong in several villages in Thailand during the 1960's (among Americans the rate is 16 per 1,000). H'mong birthrates in Laos have not been figured, but probably are similar. However, despite such a high assumed birthrate, in Laos the average household size was only about 8 persons, often comprising four adults and their children. Households as large as twenty persons could be found, but households with only a single family were not rare. For example, though over half of the households in a village studied by Lemoine contained more than one family, the rest were composed of a single family. These smaller families were at a disadvantage in farming, however.

The need to organize farm production around the men unbalanced access to decisions and choices affecting the lives of all family members. Decision-making was the domain of men because they constituted the core of the family, and the unit of decision was the family, not the individual. All family members were expected to submit to what was perceived as the overall welfare of the group.

Thus women did not enjoy a life of egalitarian freedom among the H'mong in Southeast Asia. Upon marriage, a H'mong woman moved into her husband's family and subsequently saw less and less of her own natal family. The American frontier saying, "men work from sun to sun, but women's work is never done," might equally have been said about the H'mong. Girls were raised to be hard workers, and a married woman was expected willingly to obey her husband and his parents. Good

*"A special pattern for a
New Year's skirt"* with
shells and the cats
walking around.
Mang Vang

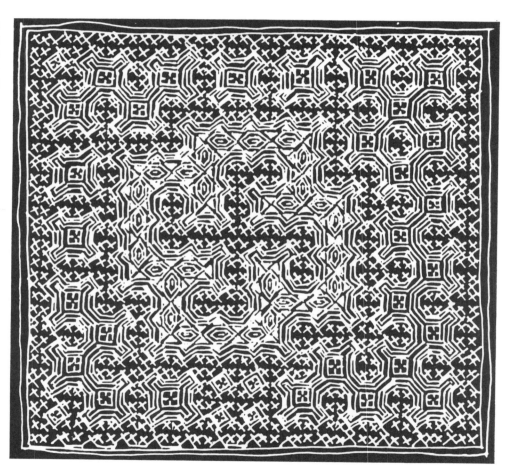

temper and work skills were the characteristics most valued in women.

It can even be said that a H'mong woman might make only one really important decision in her whole life. In choosing whom to marry, she was supposed to exercise her own free choice. The years of courtship were a H'mong girl's time in the sun. Her mother (who usually supervised her work) often gave her free time to sew elaborately beautiful costumes and to gossip, and in the evenings she and her girlfriends could receive romantic visits from young men. The New Year's celebrations were a time of formalized courtship games that let young people meet each other in groups. But a girl carefully concealed her serious attachments from her parents, who on their part carefully looked the other way. Eventually she would reach an understanding with a suitor, and willingly make the leap into marriage.

* * *

In the 1940's and 1960's, owing to new roads, in some villages the variety of goods brought by traders increased markedly, and farmers were able to sell potatoes and other crops in Hanoi. Women added new colors and materials to their needlework repertoire, using French cotton and Chinese silk floss. Protestant missionaries arrived. New Lao primary schools taught a small number of H'mong boys.

The French were defeated at Dien Bien Phu in 1954, ending the First Indochina War, and the Royal Lao Government was established. After a period of civil strife in

Variation: "many coins connected together."
Mai Ying Her

Laos, the United States began providing large amounts of aid to conservative factions there, including the H'mong. After 1960, social and economic development in Laos continued, supported by United States Agency for International Development (U.S.-AID) policies and programs.

As the Second Indochina War (Vietnam War) progressed into the 1960's, the relatively self-sufficient highland economy deteriorated, and contacts with non-H'mong necessarily expanded. Thousands of H'mong were forced to flee the highlands and congregate in large settlements. Unable to farm and frequently on the move, they were fed by American airdrops of rice and tinned meat. H'mong men joined the army in large numbers. With military funding, schools were built in the fast-growing towns, where many H'mong boys and some girls began a Lao education.

Our informants for this book were older Blue H'mong women in Washington and California who once lived in two provinces of Laos, Sayaboury and Xieng Khouang. Sayaboury Province was almost exclusively rural, having only one large town (Sayaboury) and very few roads. While they were touched by the war in Southeast Asia, the women from this area did not suffer complete disruption of their life patterns over such a long period as did the women from Xieng Khouang.

Xieng Khouang Province, on the other hand, was a major military crossroads during the war. Villages grew into cities as displaced farm families, fleeing the fighting, abandoned their fields and villages to stream into concentrated settlements.

Variation: "many coins connected together."
Mai Ying Her

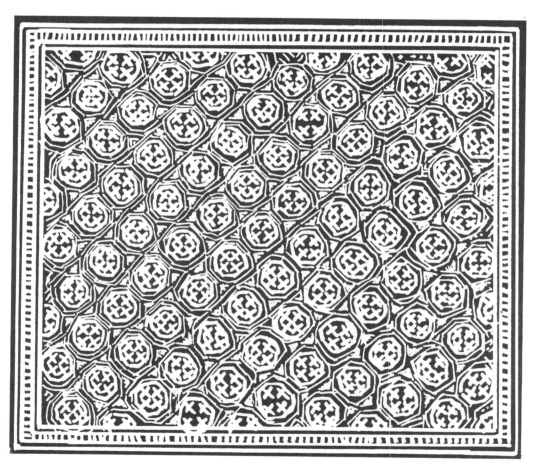

Owing to this sudden urbanization, a more complicated society was in the process of being created, with a mixed economy, the presence of many foreigners, and different relationships of power. Some soldiers' wives living in towns had leisure to produce large wardrobes; however, during the 1960's and 1970's elite and educated H'mong women tended to adopt Lao or even Western styles if they lived in cities. A very small trade developed in batiked skirts. There are many examples of H'mong women suddenly living in ways not previously possible. For example, one of our H'mong woman friends began trading on her own account, buying and selling Pepsi, chickens, vegetables, and nylon fabric. Another entered nurses' training and began flying in helicopters.

Under strong military influence, H'mong men developed deeper hierarchies of command and tried to realize long-standing ideas of a future H'mong kingdom. However, as the Pathet Lao pushed south, H'mong supporting the Royal Lao Government had to abandon more and more possessions and make frequent moves to new fall-back positions. War deaths became common for civilians as well as soldiers, and nearly everyone lost family members. Things fell apart in the chaos of losing the war, and thousands of people had to abandon their homes, their dead, their useless paper money, their animals, and their heavy, lovingly created clothing.

Some H'mong left Laos as the Royal Laotian Government fell in 1975, some went back to farming, and many others fled into the jungle. For this last group, the domestic domain completely collapsed. They were unable to farm and subsisted on

"Pattern for a baby carrier."
Mai Ying Her

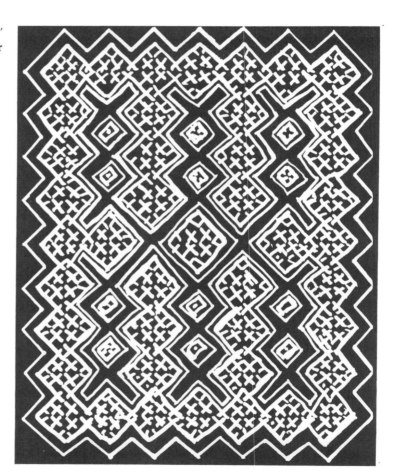

wild plants. Without trade, items like soap, salt, needles, fabric, medicines, tobacco, combs—common things of daily life—were out of reach. Hemmed in by enemies and pursuing the persistent belief that somehow they could mount an armed resistance, eventually they had nothing. The struggle to survive overwhelmed their efforts at guerrilla warfare, and starving survivors of this ill-fated effort straggled out to Thailand in 1977, 1978, and 1979. Other H'mong, who had tried to resume farming, also slipped away across the Mekong River in those years or subsequently, either to rejoin their families or to escape the very heavy taxes imposed under the new communist state.

Between 1979 and 1981, thousands of H'mong arrived in the United States without English, knowing little of American life, and disoriented by their recent harsh experiences. They had spent much more time on average than the Vietnamese in refugee camps—34 months compared with about 8 months. The H'mong had been stripped of several aspects of their former identity. Their bid for an independent territory had backfired, and political self-determination in the relative isolation of the mountains was a thing of the past. They had lost economic self-sufficiency. Yet they retained memories of these as an ethnic charter of identity in their new situation, and retained also other elements of H'mong identity, such as language and needlework skill. They still thought of themselves as clever and resilient. Their patrilineality and patriarchal social ideals had not been shaken. They had gained a reputation for alliance with the American effort that entitled them to special consideration from the

Variation: *"many coins connected together."*
Mai Ying Her

United States government. Their mutual suffering made them draw closer together, minimizing their own differences in a new and strange environment.

The H'mong Resettlement Study estimated that by 1983, 60-64,000 H'mong were living in the United States. Of this number, 28-30,000 lived in California. The figure is an estimate because of rapid natural increase (about 54,000 had been admitted to the United States at the time of the study). Small numbers of H'mong migrants continued to arrive, reunifying families split by war and flight. Today perhaps 75-80,000 or more H'mong live in this country.

Like other refugees of the Vietnam era, entering H'mong initially were scattered over the map of America. The purpose of this plan of resettlement was to minimize the impact on any single locale of a sudden influx of refugees. Like other refugees, however, as soon as they oriented themselves, H'mong immediately tried to find their relatives. They moved to cluster together for mutual material and emotional support. Eight percent of these communities have fewer than 1,000 members, while two communities have over 8,000 persons.

H'mong entering the United States were not well prepared for life in our post-industrial economy. H'mong background was predominantly rural (92% rural) and nonliterate (71% were nonliterate upon arrival). The H'mong language itself had no written form until missionaries invented a script during the 1950's; few H'mong learned this script in Laos, however. Since the best predictor of educational success for any migrant is previous education in the homeland, it is no surprise that while education

This is called "old lady pattern" because it is the pattern for an old lady's skirt and because it is said to come directly, unchanged, from earlier H'mong people in China.
La Xiong

for H'mong refugees after arrival in "survival English" averaged 1.6 years, by 1983, 34% of H'mong adults still had no English proficiency, while 50% could not read English at all. The inability of many H'mong adults to perform classroom work has nothing to do with inborn talent, but is a result of growing up where formal education was absent.

H'mong refugees in the United States have tried to set up again the household and family structures that were familiar from Laos. For instance, virtually all H'mong live in families (not as singles). Family groups consist of parents, children, and many other kinds of dependents, such as widowed mothers, unmarried brothers and sisters of the husband or wife, and unattached minors treated as relatives. Kinship ties are very flexible in H'mong society, and relationships that are objectively quite distant can be reinterpreted to seem closer, a very useful trait where so many family members are far away or have died. Still, the households composed of many nuclear families, which were found in Laos, are very rare in America. This is partly because apartments are too small, and also probably because there are no essential economic ties holding such large groups together. Income for refugees, as for Americans, is wage-based or entitlement-based, and goes to the nuclear family without consideration for attachments between families.

There is quite a bit of economic and social cooperation between households related by blood or marriage. Besides advice of all sorts, cooperation can include mutual babysitting and driving, trading clothes among sisters-in-law, finding jobs, or

"Bells ring in a circle."
La Xiong

pooling money to buy a car for someone, for weddings and for funerals, and for other sudden expenses, such as moving. Networks between related men are so strong that if a young man wants to marry or buy a car and all his male relatives disapprove, they will nonetheless produce the money for him in the face of their own anxiety and even disgust, if he insists. On the women's side ties are weaker but still present, and women often talk with their relatives every day if they live in the same city. Sons-in-law frequently give money and services to their fathers-in-law.

Authority within the H'mong household in America is more problematical than it was in Laos. With the education of young women, the increase in nuclear households, employment of wives outside the home, and a high rate of unemployment among older men who would normally carry high status, there is a leveling process that is apparent in somewhat increased decision-making by wives compared to what would have been true in Laos. The H'mong still believe that the husband is superior to the wife, and that he should be the breadwinner while she should remain in a domestic role. Therefore many women avoid working if they can, and perceive themselves as having less influence than their husbands. H'mong women who make decisions are likely to say, "My husband wants to do this," or, "This is is important for the family." Girls still often marry by age 15 and begin to build families. Thus success for most H'mong women continues to depend on motherhood and a domestic horizon.

On the other hand, a small number of H'mong women choose to divorce un-

"Coins and shells mixed up
together."
La Xiong

satisfactory husbands, and young widows may choose not to remarry. They go back to their own families or set up independent households with their children. These paths would have been virtually impossible in Laos.

Older men have trouble holding onto their prestige, particularly when they have to depend on sons or grandchildren to deal with American society. The active political and community leaders among the H'mong are nearly all in their thirties and forties, with the older men retaining control of traditional ritual, wedding negotiations, and cultural memory. Among Christianized H'mong, ritual also seems to have moved into younger hands.

Education is much valued by H'mong parents, but as many of them are without education themselves, they are unable to help their children. They exhort them to study, but cannot be sure they actually learn. Most H'mong children are average achievers in school. Some, as they enter the upper grades, adopt very Americanized attitudes of alienation from H'mong culture. While their parents remember the old ways, the children have no direct experience of Laos. If the H'mong in the second generation follow the path of most migrants to America, they will concentrate on fitting into their new environment. It will be the third generation that will want to reconstruct a remembrance of the past.

A "piece pattern" of triangles outlined in dots whose regular size and spacing show Blia Hang Yang's exceptional command of her pen and wax.
Blia Hang Yang

Textiles and H'mong Society

I n a culture like that of the traditional Blue H'mong in Laos, where the practice of slash and burn (swidden) agriculture led to frequent moves, where traditions were transmitted verbally or by encouraging imitation, the ability to recreate significant items of material culture was very valuable. Due to their semi-migratory way of life, the H'mong did not amass great quantities of material possessions. What they did develop was an acute, practical sense of the necessary and important material items for the reestablishment of correct H'mong life in each new location. The men were competent at woodworking, farming and animal husbandry, and were renowned as metalworkers. At each new village site they painstakingly recreated the houses, tools and agricultural implements required to live properly.

Likewise the women, responsible for the clothing of all family members, developed enough skill in the growing, preparing and weaving of hemp to provide the cloth for clothing and bedding. The women also learned from an early age to decorate their textiles and create clothing identifying themselves and their families as Blue H'mong, and from a particular region of Laos.

This is another pattern in which the shell motif has been abstracted to emphasize the diagonal lines of an elaborate cross-hatching, emphasized by a cross-hatch border. It is called "biting snail pattern."
Blia Hang Yang

In a life of frequent moves, textiles were an important material expression of cultural and social values. They were portable; they made an identifying statement on sight; their makers transmitted a specialized historical tradition which extended beyond the intrinsic value of the items they created. The elaborate skirts of the Blue H'mong women expressed these qualities. The women who made and wore the skirts created a material symbol not only of Blue H'mong identity, but also of a Blue H'mong woman's role in creating social bonds.

Blue H'mong social structure in Laos was similar to that of traditional Chinese society, and remains so in the United States. Families were grouped into clans, identified by surnames. Authority resided in the men, who were heads of households and clan leaders, and who were brought up to depend upon their brothers and male cousins for support and companionship throughout their lives. By contrast, the women had no formal power within either their natal families or their husbands' families. They were expected to marry outside their own clans, with the marriage negotiations controlled by their clansmen, and to become the responsiblity of the clans into which they married. In practical terms marriage for women often meant moving to a new village, breaking ties with mother, sisters, and childhood friends.

When a woman married, the wealth and importance of her family was in part expressed by the number of skirts her mother gave her to take to her new home. This number reflected the bride's own skill and industry, as some of the skirts given her were her own work. Anything she had made in her parents' home before her mar-

"Grouped snails" is unusual in that it is a pattern common in White H'mong applique but not in Blue H'mong batik. The tiny individual dots that form the whorl show the exquisite command Blia Hang Yang has over her medium, as she can manipulate her "pen" to make them in hot wax without blots.
Blia Hang Yang

riage was counted as their property, because they supplied the materials, and allowed the daughter to take time from farm or childcare responsiblities to make the batik, work the embroidery, and cut and sew the applique to complete the skirts, sashes and jackets. The family had the option of keeping back some of the daughter's work, though they rarely exercised it. In Laos, after a woman married, she was expected to create a set of clothing for her parents: ideally, a complete traditional costume for each of them. This clothing would be kept to put on the corpse when the parent died. For the woman, an important element of this clothing was the skirt which she made for her mother. It had to be at least partly of hemp cloth, the cloth of her ancestors. This skirt was understood to be given in exchange for one of the skirts given by the mother to her daughter as part of her marriage dowry. The daughter kept the dowry skirt to be worn on her own deathbed, so that when she died and "returned to China" her mother could identify her and, despite the separation created in life by H'mong social traditions, they could finally be reunited.

These exchanges of textiles by mother and daughter gave material form to an informal but important relationship between the husband and his wife's male relations. Though a man traditionally depended for help and support upon his own brothers and male relatives, his wife's family could be a secondary source of possibilities, for example, in choosing a new farming location, or in organizing labor or raising money for a project. This access to a secondary source of support in the wife's relatives continues in the United States and has been very helpful to H'mong

"A small horn pattern" uses joined snail shells and coins to create a new motif.
Blia Hang Yang

families needing money to relocate or to start businesses.

A woman's reputation as a textile artist was made among other women; to her prospective husband and his relatives her expertise was an indication of her diligence and capacity for work. In the men's world, she could give opinions, but she had no direct part in decision making. Her place as an adult was shaped by the concerns of family, home and farm; her private time could be spent making and decorating clothing with needle, thread, pen and wax.

Mothers with more money than time also bought skirts (or the batiked panels for skirts), if they felt a need to emphasize their family status vis-a-vis that of the groom's family. One of our informants, Mang, who came from a wealthy family, reported that she had nine skirts when she was married, whereas a girl from a poor family might have to be content with one or two. Mang and La Xiong reported that buying skirts was not common in Sayaboury until the 1960's, though it was probably common earlier in more cosmopolitan Xieng Khouang. Still, it is clear that the intricate batik panel was the part of a woman's skirt that she was most likely to purchase, if she knew an artist and could pay the price.

Often, when she married, a girl did not know how to sew as well as she might. She had not had the time or opportunity to learn many of the batik and embroidery patterns that her mother and her female relatives could teach her. She might not be able to weave, or to make up the indigo dye correctly. Her mother had usually started her on these skills; after her marriage, it was the responsibility of her mother-in-law,

*"A cross pattern" emphasized
with very delicate dots and a
triangle border.*
Blia Hang Yang

sometimes assisted by older sisters-in-law, to remedy any deficiencies.

The education of a bride to conform to the expectations of her husband's family was essential to the public perception of the family, and was therefore a very important responsibility both of the teacher and of the pupil. Not only did it ensure that the daughter-in-law would conform to her mother-in-law's standards, but it also provided an opportunity to establish a bond with the mother-in-law. A bride's age at marriage varied from early teens to early twenties; some younger brides needed more thorough instruction from their mothers-in-law than did the older ones.

That the batik technique and patterns were an important part of the tribal heritage handed down by a Blue H'mong woman to her daughters and daughters-in-law is illustrated by Mang Vang's experiences. She learned batik from her mother, and also from her sister-in-law, the wife of her eldest brother, a woman who married into the family when Mang was about ten years old. This sister-in-law was White H'mong, and had never learned any batik techniques or patterns as a child. According to H'mong social custom, however, she became a Blue H'mong upon her marriage, and her mother-in-law, Mang's mother, was responsible for teaching her new daughter-in-law everything she needed to know to become a proper Blue H'mong woman and an asset to her husband's family and clan. The mother-in-law taught her new daughter-in-law batik so thoroughly that this White H'mong woman became renowned as a regional batik artist, and was, in turn, instrumental in teaching her young Blue H'mong sister-in-law, Mang.

"A special pattern for a New Year's skirt" with shells and cucumber flowers.
Mang Vang

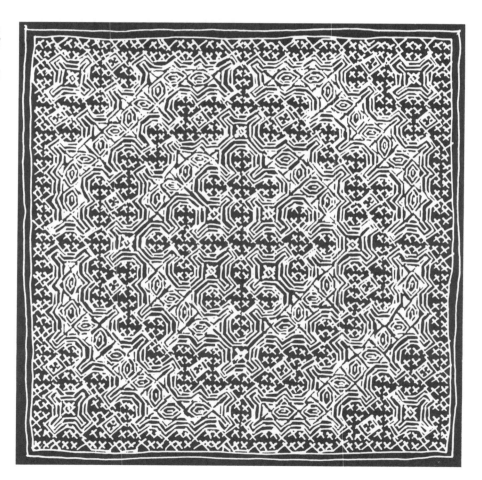

Mang herself had a similar experience after marriage, when she, age eighteen, became the wife of a man whose sister had married and moved away, and whose brothers were unmarried. In the first years of Mang's marriage, her mother-in-law concentrated on Mang's training. She taught Mang many batik patterns, but more important, Mang remembers, was the pride her mother-in-law and her husband took in her accomplishments, encouraging her to make more skirts and create more patterns rather than to devote herself totally to farm and children. Her mother-in-law took on many of Mang's household chores to allow Mang time for her batik and needlework.

This pattern is called "two coins stand up together." It also includes the festive shell motif, and has a shell border.
La Xiong

Learning To Do Batik

In their education as in their costume, Blue H'mong children were considered miniature adults, imitating adult occupations from the time they could walk. In the patrilineal-patrilocal society of the H'mong, boys were favored in all families as sources of labor and support in the parents' old age, above the girls who were bound to marry and move away. Boys learned from their fathers, uncles and older brothers to build, farm and hunt. But while the men transmitted a wide range of material knowledge, textile technique was the only part of a woman's knowledge which was expressed in durable materials. Her mother or grandmother was responsible for introducing a girl to the domestic skills which would make her marriageable. Performance as a farmworker was evidence of a girl's health and strength; from her earliest childhood she cared for her younger siblings, but a girl's performance as a needlewoman was visible evidence that she had been brought up to respect and follow the traditions of H'mong life.

There was perhaps another incentive for learning. In her mother's daily activities—tending animals, working in the fields, caring for children (with particular

This is a variation on the divorce pattern, slightly more elaborate, dressed up with shells to make it suitable for a New Year's skirt.
La Xiong

concentration on the male children)—there was little opportunity for a small daughter to get the concentrated attention of her mother (or of any adult woman) and to create a bond. One of the few opportunities came while learning textile skills.

A Blue H'mong girl learned to do cross-stitch embroidery from an early age, copying patterns from her mother or other female relatives. At the age of ten or twelve she began to learn applique (sewing pieces of cloth in contrasting colors onto the background material of a skirt, for example), again working alongside her mother, sisters and sisters-in-law, copying from clothing in the family. Blue H'mong girls did not learn reverse applique (in which a pattern is cut in a piece of material, and the edges of the cuts are turned under and stitched down to a fabric of contrasting color, so that the background material shows through the appliqued material), which was a specialty of White H'mong, though many have learned how to do it since moving to the Thai refugee camps or coming to America. Embroidery and applique were portable, social skills. Girls took pleasure in sewing their festive skirts in sociable groups, exchanging patterns, building friendships, gossiping and looking forward to the New Year's harvest festival, when, dressed in their best, they might meet their future husbands.

The last decorative skill a Blue H'mong girl learned was batik, in some ways the most difficult for the finickiness of its technique. Learning to do batik required considerably more interest, patience and application than learning embroidery or applique. Unlike the other techniques, which could readily be picked up and put down,

This is the "pattern of the grandmother, the pattern a grandmother would make to give to a small child." The motifs are large and the pattern is regular and solid, suitable perhaps for the failing eyesight of an elderly woman or the first waxing attempts of a young child.
La Xiong

batik involved commitment of a block of time, and total concentration within the time allowed. It involved more variables than the other techniques, and more specialized equipment. To make even a simple pattern, a woman had to assemble the materials: cloth, beeswax, a way to melt it, at least one pen; and there had to be some dye available. Because of the complexity of the patterns, and the concentration necessary to remember them, batik was a solitary activity, and a woman might arrange to have her housekeeping and childcare done by another relative so she could complete her skirt.

To have proper clothes for everyday farm work as well as a new skirt for each New Year celebration, and to make skirts for their daughters, Blue H'mong women had various strategies to cut the long time necessary to complete each skirt. Those with sufficient means could buy batik-decorated skirt lengths, or even completely finished skirts from regional artists. But most women learned at least a few of the batik patterns which were known for being easy and quick (for example, the "divorce" pattern and the "fern" border pattern seen on page 62). Many women stayed at this level of work, but those who were more interested in learning went on to become batik artists, each with a repertoire of intricate patterns and a local reputation. A batik artist was a potential economic asset to her family (while her eyesight remained good enough for the exacting work) if her husband would allow her to make batik skirt lengths for sale. An acknowledged regional batik artist could command a price as high (according to one woman) as twenty pieces of silver, or (according to

"Crossroads and coins."
Mai Ying Her

another), the equivalent of five days' farm labor in Sayaboury during the 1960's, for a batik skirt length of twenty-five to thirty pattern blocks.

This pattern shows a crossroads; it is made up of coins and pumpkin flowers, with cat foot-prints through the back-ground and around the edge. This is a quick pattern, easy to make, and often used for an everyday skirt. It might be used for a New Year's skirt if one were in a hurry.
Mang Vang

Textiles As Costume: Women's Dress

Costume provided an important aspect of identity to the many different ethnic groups of Southeast Asia, who set themselves apart from one another at a glance by the style and decorative details of their clothing, and the Laotian H'mong were no exception. From their earliest arrival as refugees in the United States, H'mong women were distinguished by their intricate and colorful needlework. H'mong women seen today on American streets dress as much like American women as they can, so as not to look conspicuous in their new surroundings, to avoid stares on the bus or comments in the streets. This reserve and concentration on conformity with the prevailing social norms, expressed here in costume, has been characteristic of H'mong attitudes for generations. As they express their new public American selves in their American clothing, so in their native Laos these women expressed their public H'mong selves by making and wearing clothing distinctive in outline, color, decoration and style.

The Blue H'mong women's costume, worn for both everyday and ceremonies, consisted of a narrow-sleeved jacket, open or crossed in the front, a turban-like head-

"Short cut" is a "cross" pattern with spaces left for applique on the finished panel. This is the design most often employed for baby carriers.
Blia Hang Yang

dress, and the knee-length pleated skirt, tied around the waist and left open in the front. The opening was covered by a narrow apron attached to a long sash, which was wound twice around the waist and knotted in the back. Finally, leggings were wrapped like puttees around the lower legs, and the feet were usually left bare, except on festive occasions, when women whose families could afford them might wear shoes bought from the Chinese trader in the village or from a local market.

The costume was well-suited to the activities of daily life. It could also be adapted easily to the changing climate of high mountain ranges. The jacket could be opened easily to feed a baby, or to cool the upper body. The narrow sleeves left the hands free even when the wearer was bent over in the fields, planting or weeding or harvesting. The headdress kept the hair out of the face. The leggings protected the lower legs from forest undergrowth and from loose stones in the path. And the skirt allowed freedom of movement over rough ground, or when stooping or squatting in the course of household work. In the latter case, the apron which closed the front of the skirt dropped neatly between the legs to ensure that the wearer was completely covered. Girls and women wore the same styles, though less work and material would be used on clothes which would soon be outgrown by a child. Only the headgear was different; babies and small children wore elaborate, colorful hats in different styles for boys and girls. Small children were carried on the backs of mothers or older sisters in a baby carrier, a cloth sling worn like a backpack. This baby carrier was the only item of clothing besides the skirt which had batik decoration.

Called "open, connecting links" this pattern reflects the connections of the H'mong people to their clans, their families and each other.
La Xiong

The Making of a Batik Skirt

In Laos, embroidery and applique were techniques that depended, as they do now in the United States, upon materials such as colored cloth, ribbons, and thread bought in shops or from wandering traders. But batik did not depend on outside sources. Batik decoration of hemp cloth produced an unique, idiosyncratic material entirely without assistance from outside the home. It was a decorative technique which used only material either grown on the farm (hemp and indigo) or gathered in the forest (beeswax). Only the copper for the pens came from the outside world.

1. Making the Thread

Hemp was a cultivated crop on each farm in Laos, so that each family could make enough cloth for itself. The first step in the production of thread was growing the hemp from which the thread was made. The seed was sown in a patch, broadcast in one section of a field, rather than being planted in rows. After a month or more, the plants were cut, the leaves were stripped off, and the stalks were left to dry in the

"Design from a Chinese bowl."
La Xiong

sun. There were always some very tall and tough plants on the outside edge of the patch, plants which had not had to struggle against the other plants to grow. These were too tough for thread, so they were allowed to go to seed. The seed was carefully saved for the next crop, while the bundles of stalks were stored in the house to keep dry until needed.

Then the bark was peeled from the stalks to get fiber. The night before this process was to start, some stalks would be put outside to become damp and soft in the dew, so they would be easier to peel. The peeling took a long time and was very hard on the hands. According to Ly Hang, a woman's husband should help her peel the bark off the stalks. They could work on this at night, when the day's farm chores were done. Even if he did not help in the peeling, the husband should take care of the children so that the wife would be free to work, and he should also stay awake after dinner and keep his wife company while she worked on the hemp (or, later, on the batik decoration itself) so that she wouldn't be scared in the night.

When the bark was peeled, the fibers were gathered into bundles, and the women twisted the ends together, joining the separate fibers into a continuous thread. Women often worked at this while walking back and forth between the village and their fields. They would push a bundle of fibers about the diameter of a thumb and finger circle under one shoulder strap of their packbaskets, and pull out one fiber at a time as they walked along, twisting each new piece onto the end of the previous one

*"Coins going different ways,
with shells."*
La Xiong

and winding the completed thread into a figure-eight between thumb and little finger over the back of their hands.

These skeins of fiber were pale green, the color of the bark. They were bleached white by successive boilings in water to which wood ash had been added. After each boiling, the fibers were lifted out of the pot, wrapped in large leaves, and taken to the river, where the ash was removed by washing the fibers and beating them on the river rocks, then drying them in the sun. This process was repeated until the thread was as white as necessary.

Once the thread was coiled and bleached, it was spun to give it a twist, and then the weaving could begin. Again, a woman's husband could help with the preparation of the thread, and he made all the pieces of the wooden spinning wheel and loom, but when it came time to warp the loom, men were excluded from the process. Ly Hang says that if a man were to help or even watch the process, the threads would not be straight, and it would be impossible to get a good, tight piece of cloth.

2. Cloth for the Skirt

In Laos the heavy batik skirts were commonly made in three horizontal panels of hemp cloth: the hip panel, the batik panel, and the hem panel. The upper hip panel, attached to the waistband and ending at the top of the hip, was made of plain white or indigo dyed cloth. The central batik panel, usually extending from the top of

"Connect the coins together"
with a border of flowers and
mountains.
La Xiong

the hip to the knee, was made of the intricately batik-decorated hemp cloth. In the 1960's, as hill farming became more profitable for the Blue H'mong, cotton cloth bought in a market was used for the batik panel. Most of the skirts we have seen have a third panel, the hem panel, which extends from the bottom of the batik panel to the hem of the skirt, just below the wearer's knees. A few of the old skirts dating from the 1930's and 40's were simply finished with a row or two of cross stitch along the bottom of the batik panel rather than having a separate hem panel.

Tailoring of the skirts was quite difficult, and highly personalized, as the average length of material in an adult skirt was about eight yards, all of which was compressed into a waistband of about thirty-two inches by means of very fine and tight pleats. The measurements depended upon the spread of the wearer's thumb and first finger, and upon the spread of her outstretched arms. The width of the batik panel (in a skirt with a separate hem panel) was two thumb and finger spreads; its length, four times the wearer's outstretched arms. The hip panel was one thumb and finger spread; the waistband, four thumb and finger spreads around, with longer ends left for tying. The hem panel was traditionally rather narrow, extending from the bottom of the batik panel to just below the wearer's knee. Our informants noted that as trade with lowland villages increased in the 1960's and 1970's, allowing access to money for more embroidery threads and a wider variety of colors, the embroidered hem panels began to get wider at the expense of the batik, and became in their turn a marker of family wealth. When fitting the finished skirt, the maker carefully adjusted the pleats to lie smoothly on the hip and at the back, so that the hem would hang evenly all around.

3. Decorating the Batik Panel

The designs were drawn on homespun hemp or bought cotton cloth. The cotton was preferred because it had a smoother surface than the hemp and fine lines could be more easily drawn on it, so the final design would be very clear and elegant. It was also lighter in weight than the hemp, so the finished skirt was more comfortable to wear, especially during rainy weather when the weight of a wet skirt was considerable. Because of its expense, cotton cloth was used at first only for the batik panels; all-cotton skirts were not common in Laos until the 1970's.

The designs were created by applying a resist of hot beeswax to the cloth using a triangular copper pen held in a distinctive manner, allowing precise control of the flow of wax to produce the even lines necessary for the geometric designs of the traditional patterns. The best wax for the purpose was a mixture of new beeswax with beeswax which had been recovered from the rinse water of previous batik. This old wax retained some of the blue color from the indigo dye, and made the patterns easier to see on the white cloth. It was also said to make the new wax more workable. The wax was melted and kept hot during the drawing in a small pot over the fire.

The H'mong batik pen in use.
M. Davidson

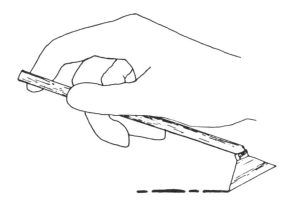

Some women used the same pen throughout the waxing process, and produced excellent detailed work reflecting years of practice in maneuvering the instrument. Many of the acknowledged artists, however, had a collection of pens of varying thicknesses, achieved by different numbers of copper leaves (see page 63). These pens would make thicker or thinner lines, as they held a larger or smaller reserve of wax in the space between the leaves. Certain pens were used for the long lines of the border, different ones for the longer lines within the pattern, different again for the

This drawing shows the layout of the pattern on the cloth for a skirt length. The top border is a pattern of teeth enclosing a fern pattern, sometimes also called "mountain."

The lower border is a stylized shell pattern. The left vertical divider is a triangle pattern, while the right is the fern pattern again.

The square itself is worked in a crossroads pattern. Because she was using a pen with a very fine point to draw on the paper, the artist here indicated the long lines in the pattern with two lines, where there would be a single, thicker line of wax on the cloth, resulting in a long, white line on the final skirt. For example, the border of teeth at the top of the skirt would appear on a finished skirt as a solid white line with one jagged edge, not as the two thin lines, one jagged, which appear here.

Mang Vang

crosshatching and the dots.

A H'mong batik pen with a copper head and a bamboo handle, showing the arrangement of the leaves of copper which serve as a reservoir of wax for the pen.
M. Davidson

The wax design was applied to the batik panel as shown on page 62. The cloth was rolled into a scroll, with one end fastened to a board as wide as the material and about three feet long. As the work progressed, the cloth was moved along the board, with the finished part being rolled up out of the way, and the unwaxed portion being fastened to the board one section at a time. The design was laid out with borders at the upper and lower edges running the full length of the piece. The lines for these were

A variation on the crossroads, this pattern is called "a cross that whirls" like a pinwheel. La Xiong was a teacher of Mang Vang when they were young married women living in the same village in Laos. Her patterns appear differently here from the way they would appear on a skirt length in that she has done just a small piece of each, and finished it with an elaborate border, to provide us with what she understood as samples. In a skirt length, the overall pattern would be more extensively developed, and the visual importance of the border would be secondary to the central pattern in the whole design.
La Xiong

This pattern ("a cross that whirls" from the previous page) has been dissected here to show how the wax is typically applied in making a batik design.
M. Davidson

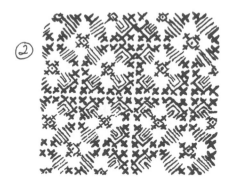

drawn in wax the full length of the cloth, using a board as a straight edge. Next, the space was divided into squares by using vertical lines to create shorter border sections. The skirt length was now divided into a series of large squares. A typical skirt length had twenty-five to thirty of these squares. These large squares were in turn subdivided into smaller squares. This was done by scoring the cloth with a blunt instrument such as the back of a knife or a stick. Then each large square was filled in with a particular pattern, applied directly in wax, using the small scored squares as a reference grid. First the upper and lower borders were filled in, then the vertical dividers. Finally the large squares were filled in using either a traditional pattern throughout or traditional motifs arranged according to the artist's taste.

For each pattern square, the wax was applied with an elegant economy of gesture. With the finished pattern in mind, the artist waxed all the lines in a given direction on the finished square. Then she turned the work, and applied the next set of lines, building up the pattern through increasingly elaborate crosshatching until the final design became clear. At this point the cloth was ready for dyeing.

4. Patterns

The patterns used to complete the squares were drawn from each woman's repertoire, learned over time from friends and relatives. They were variations upon, or copies of, patterns which the H'mong believe to have originated generations previously in China, their ancestral home. Some patterns were dense with motifs, others were more sketchy in character, with blank spaces purposely left to be filled in with cotton applique in bright contrasting colors on the finished skirts. There was some general variation between patterns from the northern province of Sayaboury, the home of one group of informants, and the southern province of Xieng Khouang, home of the other group. Sayaboury was a source of dense patterns, with many motifs grouped in various ways, and very little space left in the design itself for applique. The Xieng Khouang skirts often had isolated motifs in a field left open for applique. This variation perhaps reflected the greater prosperity·of the south, with its exposure to the colors and styles of the capital at Vientiane.

In Sayaboury, a less wealthy and more conservative region, the batik tradition was truer to the intricate drawing of the Chinese heritage, possibly because there was less money and opportunity to buy thread and cloth for elaborate applique. Sayaboury tradition still dictated in the 1960's that a batik panel must never be decorated with applique. To do so on a skirt intended for one's mother would be to wish her stony ground in her new life after death, rather than the fertile fields of an ideal farm. Once, we were told, all the patterns had traditional names and stories associated with them, but our informants did not tell us such stories. To us, there seem to be as many names and interpretations of patterns as there are women trying to remember them.

The individual motifs of the patterns reflected the village and farm life of the H'mong. As the captions of individual patterns show, there were stylized pumpkin flowers, squash flowers, cats' footprints, coins, mountains (sometimes called teeth), and shells, and some pathways through the village. It was important to H'mong women to learn the patterns exactly as they were taught, but a woman could make a pattern of her own, we were told, by changing one motif in one corner of the square.

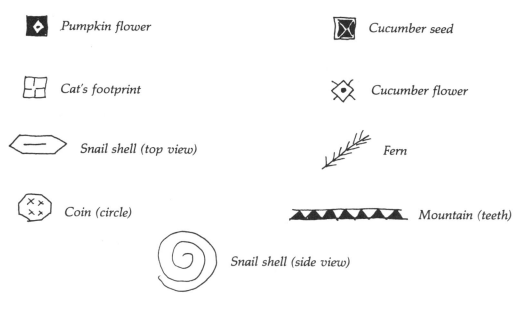

Pumpkin flower

Cucumber seed

Cat's footprint

Cucumber flower

Snail shell (top view)

Fern

Coin (circle)

Mountain (teeth)

Snail shell (side view)

The cotton or rayon for applique, bought from Chinese traders in the villages or from lowland markets, was traditionally red, but from the early 1960's, as larger farm incomes led to more demand and more varied supply, the color range expanded to include yellow, hot pink and lime green.

5. Dyeing the Batik Panel

The process of making the blue dye for the waxed cloth was as long and involved as the waxing of the skirt itself. The dye could sometimes be bought in the market, or from another woman, but it was traditionally made by each family. Ly Hang, the Blue H'mong collaborator on this book, describes making the dye as it was done in her family household in Laos when she was a child. It was made from three substances in a long process.

Each household had a large copper cauldron for dyeing fabric. In it, the leafy branches of an indigo plant were soaked for about a week in cold water. Then the leaves and branches were thrown away, and the water preserved. The leaves turned the water blue, but the blue shade was not considered very pretty at this point.

Next, the women took a very common soft, chalky, bluish stone, called "helping-blue-rock" (limestone), and heated it until it turned white in an open fire. The hot rocks were removed from the fire with tongs and flung into cold water, where the stones shattered and dissolved into a fine, floury powder which formed a sediment at the bottom of the container. The water was drained off and the sludge was kept. This white sediment would become the dye at the end of the process. It could be used wet immediately, or dried and saved for the future. To save it, Ly Hang's mother used to cut single joints of elephant bamboo, which grows as large as six inches in diameter. She would pack the wet sediment into these "cans" and stack them in a corner, where the stone dried out in a couple of weeks. Then the caked powder could be crumbled for use whenever dyeing was done.

When dyeing was to be done, this whitish stone-powder was added to blue water from indigo plants and stirred for a long time. About two pounds of powder was added to a twenty-gallon cauldron of the water. The stone was measured approximately, using a dipper cut from a gourd, which was also used for stirring.

Ly Hang remembers with distaste that as a little girl she used to lean over the cauldron, reaching into the water to lift and turn and stir the stone. Her skin absorbed the developing dye so that her hands and arms became deep blue, a color that would last three or four weeks no matter how hard she scrubbed.

After being stirred about an hour, the water would thicken and slow, plopping bubbles would begin to break the surface. Then the stirring could stop. The dye-stone at this point had turned a beautiful shade of blue, taking the color from the water. After sitting for a few days, the dye settled to the bottom of the cauldron (the H'mong said "it sleeps on the bottom"). The water was then drained off and discarded, and the dye was saved. Once again, it could be used immediately or stored in elephant bamboo "cans" to dry.

To prepare the dye for use, a woman took a shallow basket about two feet across, and lined it with material so it would act like a sieve. She packed wood ashes against the inside of the basket. Any sort of wood could be used to make these ashes. The amount of ash used was roughly related to the amount of water that would be used. The basket was held above the dyeing cauldron and water was poured through it, soaking through the ashes and dripping out into the cauldron. The dye powder was mixed with a small amount of cold water, and then added to the ash water in the cauldron.

Using a long, flat piece of wood, perhaps three fingers wide and four feet long, the woman stirred the ash water to mix the dye well. This was a critical step, never left to children. Gradually the color of the dye improved, and at a certain point it was ready. It took a long time to learn how to recognize this point. Stirring stopped, and the dye was left overnight, after which it was ready for use.

The dye water was cold, so that the beeswax on the fabric wouldn't dissolve. Several pieces of fabric could be dyed at one time. Supporting the material on strips of bamboo, the women dipped and lifted and redipped the material. Then they spread out the fabric carefully in the sun, watching and turning it so it damp-dried without melting the wax. The pieces were then dipped again, and the process was repeated until all light areas were gone, and the fabric appeared entirely dark.

The women made a party of the dyeing, which usually took two days. At last, when the fabric was dark enough, they left the fabric to dry in the sun for five to ten days. The sunshine fixed the dye, Ly Hang says, so that it would not fade.

At this point, the dye could be discarded unless the fabric was going to be redyed after the wax had been removed. This double-dyeing was sometimes done by women who did not like the sharp contrast of the white pattern with the dark blue background, or who wanted to demonstrate their great skill in waxing an intricate pattern.

Two kinds of double-dyeing were practiced. The simpler version was first to remove the wax by dipping the fabric in hot water, and then to redip the fabric once or twice in the dye, producing a pale blue pattern on a dark blue ground. A more complex and elegant version was to remove the wax, and then to rewax with two thin lines in the white pattern, before redyeing and redipping the cloth in hot water to remove the wax. The end result of this second process was a thin, pale blue line highlighting the center of the white pattern on the dark blue ground. This second version of the process was extremely delicate and time consuming, requiring special artistry. It was reserved for special efforts, for festival skirts or baby carrier panels, and was greatly admired as evidence of the maker's superior skill.

6. Hem Panel of the Skirt

While the batik panel was a measure of a woman's skill at the most difficult of domestic arts, the hem panel served both as a public marker of regional style and family wealth, and as an example of skill and industry. Cross-stitch embroidery was the first decorative technique learned by young H'mong girls. It was done on hemp cloth, or, later, on coarsely woven cotton. As the patterns were laid out by counting threads, a coarse weave made the best template for embroidery. Though it required good eyesight and an ability to count, embroidery did not require the patience and control of batik. Girls worked on embroidery while walking along paths, or in the intervals of farm work. The size and colors of the finished panel depended on the family's ability to buy colored thread and cloth for embroidery and applique, so the width and intricacy of the hem panel reflected the amount of money and time spent on it.

Recent Developments and Innovations in Blue H'mong Skirts

In Laos, from the 1960's on, some photosilkscreen batik lengths were available in markets. They consisted of one or two patterns repeated over and over, printed in black on blue cotton cloth. These were often used for small girls' skirts, as their use instead of hand-drawn batik allowed an enormous saving in time and effort. They were also used in some adult skirts, for their novelty, and for the speed with which the skirts could be made up. These lengths, which look tawdry to Western eyes comparing them to hand-drawn ones, were admired by some H'mong women as the patterns were very small and the motifs very clear, two highly desirable characteristics of finished batik.

As noted above, machine-woven cotton cloth became increasingly available as the hill-farming H'mong generated more cash through increasing trade with lowland markets. Indigo dye could also be bought. Some H'mong moved to urban employment in Laos, and created a demand for skirt lengths bought from acknowledged artists, and for skirts tailored by people outside the family. The elaborately appliqued skirts of Xieng Khouang became fashionable outside the borders of the province. This trend, which started in Laos before the H'mong fled, continued in the refugee camps in Thailand, where many women were exposed to the new regional styles and patterns, some of which they incorporated into their own traditions. The trend persists in the United States, where Blue H'mong and also White H'mong wear elaborate batik- and applique-decorated skirts whose style proclaims that they are H'mong in America.

Even as this happens, the techniques which made these textiles possible are being abandoned in America in favor of skills and occupations such as housecleaning or machine sewing more likely to make their practitioners a living in the new land. Since becoming refugees, many H'mong women have been encouraged by missionaries and other social service providers to adapt their needlework skills to the production of items appealing to Western taste and pocketbooks. These efforts have met with limited financial success, providing at best a supplementary source of income, though they do serve to maintain some traditional skills. In efforts to speed up production of the highly labor-intensive items, many H'mong women have begun to abandon the most complex techniques, notably batik, which were basic to the traditional textiles. Batik skirt lengths, for example, are most often imported from H'mong still in refugee camps in Thailand. Nevertheless, as the H'mong establish themselves in the United States, preserving the artistic traditions of their former life is a large part of their current identity, and we very much hope that the next generations will be able to incorporate the past in a productive future.

Story: The Origin of Batik

There lived a man and his wife and young daughter. One day the wife said to the husband that they needed a cow to sacrifice. Unfortunately the man arose late and when he arrived at the place where cows were for sale he found that there were none left. He went back home, placed a rope around his wife's neck, and beat her. She turned into a cow. She was kept in the garden where other livestock was kept until time to sacrifice her.

Meanwhile the man had married a second wife. She also had a daughter. The first daughter had to do all of the work for the family, and in addition she had to sew *pa'ndau*. She managed to do everything and sew beautifully. One day the second wife followed her to the area where the cow was kept and discovered that the cow would turn back into the mother and sew for the girl. The second wife didn't like this as the girl was getting a reputation for being clever and hardworking and her own daughter was not.

The second wife made believe she was very sick. She told the husband that he would have to sacrifice the cow so she would be well again. She had told the spirit doctor her problem and when the husband consulted him he told the husband to sacrifice the cow. The husband was distressed as he didn't want to sacrifice his first wife. He decided he would go to the big rock and ask advice from it. His second wife hid behind the rock and when she heard him ask for advice she told him to kill the cow.

The cow had heard of the plan from the spirits. She told her daughter to bring water from the stream and pour it over the ground so that it would be slippery and she would fall down and kill herself. She was afraid her husband would use an axe and this would be painful. She told her daughter not to eat any of the meat that they would cook and just to take the head, feet and tail and place them in the house where the smoke of the fire would dry and preserve them. She would then always be there for her daughter if she needed her.

When the time came for the next New Year festival the second wife decided that she would only take her own daughter as there was a very eligible young man she wanted her to marry. The first daughter was left at home cleaning and separating the mouse turds from the rice kernels. The girl was very sad and sat in the house crying. The cow's head spoke up and told her to go to the animal pen and there she would find a new outfit of clothing including a beautiful newly embroidered skirt. She could go to the festival by jumping up in the air, but she had to return before sunset. The girl was very happy. The handsome and eligible man was very attracted to her and everyone thought her beautiful although they did not recognize her in her new outfit. The first day she jumped back home before sunset and even though the man searched for her far and wide he could not find her. All he saw in the house was the dirty little girl separating the mouse turds from the rice.

On the second day, the young woman went to the New Year's festival again, and again the handsome and eligible man followed her around. When it was just about sunset she again went to leave the party and go home. The man was expecting this and he stepped on her foot. When he arrived at the house he noticed her footprint was there and he recognized her. He had found her. He asked her to marry him. The stepmother was very angry. She wanted the man to marry her own daughter. She tried to think of ways to arrange it. She cooked very good food for her daughter and the man and very bad food for her stepdaughter. The man switched his food and gave it to the stepdaughter, and ate her bad food himself.

The stepmother offered her daughter's bed to the man but he changed it around so that he slept in the bed with the stepdaughter. The stepmother stole into the room of her stepdaughter and placed wax on the eyes. Unfortunately the person in the bed was her own daughter so she put wax on her eyes by mistake.

In the early morning the man and the stepdaughter arose very early and ran off. As the sun rose the stepmother sat outside the house talking to herself. "Oh, my daughter is far away now with the handsome man." The daughter popped out of the house and said, "I am here, *nia*." The mother was furious. She sent her daughter after the pair to find and kill them. She gave her daughter a new set of clothing to exchange with the stepdaughter. "After she has a child, change clothes with her. Tell her how much you miss her and how you want to exchange clothing. When she puts on the new skirt she will die."

The daughter followed them for several years. One day she found them. The husband and young son were out fishing. The daughter did as her mother told her and exchanged clothing. The stepsister dropped dead and was buried. When the husband and son came home they said, "Hello, sister." "I am not your sister, I am your wife," she answered. The boy said, "Where is my real mother? My mother was very beautiful and she had long hair. Yours is short." After the husband went out again the sister asked the young boy what his mother did to make his father happy. The boy told her that his mother used to spread her hair out and make a pillow of it so that his father could rest his head when he was tired. "How can I have long hair like your mother?" she inquired. The boy told her to boil a huge pot of water and wet her hair, and comb it near the boiling pot. She followed his instructions and when she bent over the pot to comb her hair he pushed her in and covered the pot with the lid.

Meanwhile a tree had grown where the sister had buried the stepsister. One day an old couple in the village cut down the tree for firewood. The first wife rose up out of the smoke. The young boy was overjoyed to see his mother. She went back to the house and without knowing took the top off the pot into which the boy had pushed her stepsister. The spirit of the sister came out of the pot in the form of a black bird.

The family of three tried to run away from the village but the black bird followed them and made a big storm rage over them so that they could not travel far. They were tired and despairing. "In this life we have not had good luck," they said. "We have had a lot of suffering and pain." They decided that they had had enough. The son was turned into a lovely little hummingbird, the mother became the honeycomb and the father the hemp. When the son was hungry he could go to the mother for food. When the hummingbird goes to the honeycomb even the bees move away.

The father was the hemp which was used to weave the cloth. The mother contributed the wax to make the patterns of batik on the cloth. The couple and their child could no longer be separated; they were joined together forever.

Batik is important to the H'mong family. H'mong families are strong and tied together just as the batik is strong and cannot be destroyed. H'mong women are speaking through their families.

Note: This story was recounted by Ia Moua Yang to Patricia Symonds in Providence, Rhode Island in 1985. Ia Moua Yang considers herself a mixture of Blue and White H'mong. She comes from a White H'mong family but is married to a Blue H'mong and follows Blue H'mong tradition. The story is used with permission.

Bibliography for Further Reading

Adams, Marie Jeanne. "System and Meaning in East Sumba Textile Design: A Study in Traditional Indonesian Art." *Southeast Asia Cultural Report Series #16*. New Haven: Yale University, 1969.

Adams, Monni. "Dress and Design in Highland Southeast Asia: the Hmong (Miao) and the Yao." *Textile Museum Journal*, vol. 4, no. 1. Washington, D.C., 1974.

Abadie, Maurice. *Les Races du Haut-Tonkin de Phong-Tho a Lang-Son.* Paris: Societe d'Editions Geographique, Maritimes et Coloniales, 1924.

Bernatzik, Hugo Adolf. *Akha and Miao: Problems of Applied Ethnography in Farther India.* New Haven: Human Relations Area File, 1970 [1947].

Buhler, Alfred. "Die reservenusterungen: Versuch einer zusammenfassenden Betrachtung ihrer Technik, Entstehung und Herkunft." *Acta Tropica*, III, pp. 242-271, 1946.

Buhler, Alfred. "Handverfarbeitung und Batik bei den Meau in Nordthailand." *Ethnologische Zeitschrift*, I, pp. 61-81. Zurich: 1972.

Butler-Diaz, Jaqueline. *Yao Design of Northern Thailand.* Revised edition. Bangkok: The Siam Society, 1981.

Cain, Mead. "Women's Status and Fertility in Developing Countries: Son Preference and Economic Security." *World Bank Staff Working Paper #682, Population and Development Series #17*. Washington, D.C.: The World Bank, 1984.

Campbell, Margaret; Pongnoi, Nakoum; and Voraphitak, Chusak. *From the Hands of the Hills.* Second edition. Hong Kong: Media Transasia, 1981.

De Beauclair, Inez. "Tribal Cultures of Southwest China." *Asian Folklore and Social Life Monographs*, vol. II. Taipei: The Orient Cultural Service, 1974.

Donnelly, Nancy D.; Mallinson, Jane; Collins-Yager, Corinne; and Hang, Ly. *Research on H'mong Women.* Collaborative project funded by The Social Science Research Council of New York. Unpublished. 1984-85.

Dunnigan, Timothy. "Antecedents of Hmong Resettlement in the United States." From: *Hmong Art: Tradition and Change.* Sheboygan: John Michael Kohler Arts Center, 1985.

Geddes, William. *Migrants of the Mountains.* Oxford: Clarendon Press, 1976.

Hurlich, Marshall; and Donnelly, Nancy D. "Markers of Hmong Identity in the United States." Paper presented at the American Anthropological Association Annual Meeting, 19 November 1984, in Denver.

John Michael Kohler Arts Center. *Hmong Art: Tradition and Change.* Sheboygan: Kohler Arts Center, 1986.

Lee, Gary Yia. "The Socio-Economy of the White Hmong." Unpublished dissertation, University of Sydney, 1981.

Lemoine, Jacques. *Un Village Hmong Vert du Haut Laos: Milieu, technique, et organisation sociale.* Paris: Editions du Centre National de la Recherche Scientifique, 1972.

Lewis, Paul; and Lewis, Elaine. *Peoples of the Golden Triangle: Six Tribes in Thailand.* New York: Thames and Hudson, 1984.

Lu, Pu. *Designs of Chinese Indigo Batik.* New York: Lee Publishers Group, Inc., 1981.

Mickey, Margaret Portia. *The Cowrie Shell Miao of Kweichow.* Papers of the Peabody Museum of American Archaelogy and Ethnology, Harvard University, vol. XXXiii, no. 1. Cambridge: The Peabody Museum, 1947.

Mottin, Fr. Jean. *History of the Hmong.* Bangkok: Odean Bookstore, 1980.

Office of Refugee Resettlement. *The Hmong Resettlement Study.* Washington, D.C.: United States Department of Health and Human Services, 1985.

Rumbaut, Ruben; and Weeks, John R. "Fertility and Adaptation: Indochinese Refugees in the United States." *International Migration Review,* XX(2), pp. 428-466, 1986.

Savina, Fr. F. M. *Histoire des Miao.* Hong Kong: Imprimerie de la Societe des Mission-Etrangeres, 1930.

Sharp, Ruth B. "Tribal Arts and Crafts in Northern Thailand." From: *A Report on the Tribal Peoples in Chiengrai Province North of the Mae Kok River.* Hanks, Lucien, et al., Bennington-Cornell Anthropological Survey of Hill Tribes in Thailand. Bangkok: The Siam Society, 1964.

Steinmann, Alfred. "Batiks." *CIBA Review,* no. 58, pp. 2090-2125, 1947.

Steinmann, Alfred. "Das Batiken in China: Zur Verbrietung der Batiktechnik in China und in den angrenzenden Gebieten." *Sinologica,* II(2), pp. 105-126, 1949.

Taft, Julia Vadala; North, David S.; and Ford, David A. *Refugee Resettlement in the U.S.: Time for a New Focus.* Washington, D.C.: New TransCentury Foundation, 1979.

The Authors

Ly Hang is a Blue H'mong woman leader with experience in commercial activities in Laos. As a refugee in the United States, she founded H'mong Women's Needlecraft Association, a successful sales cooperative in Seattle. She has also designed clothing incorporating H'mong traditional patterns for the American market. She now lives and sells needlework in Detroit.

Nancy Donnelly is finishing her Ph.D. dissertation in Anthropology at the University of Washington. Her subject is H'mong women's adaptations to American society. She has studied H'mong language and history. Currently she is Assistant Director of the Northwest Regional Center for Southeast Asian Studies in Seattle.

Jane Mallinson became interested in H'mong textiles as a volunteer with the H'mong Women's Assistance Project. She has completed her Master's thesis in Anthropology at the University of Washington, studying techniques and patterns of Blue H'mong batik. She lives in Seattle and continues to collect batik patterns.